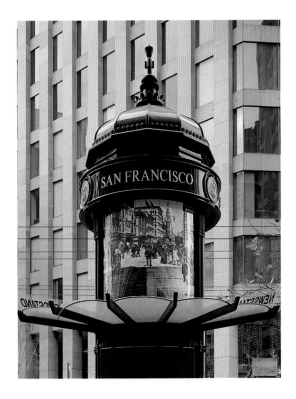

CAROL M. HIGHSMITH AND TED LANDPHAIR

SAN FRANCISCO

A PHOTOGRAPHIC TOUR

CRESCENT BOOKS

NEW YORK

FRONT COVER:
The strait into San
Francisco Bay was
called the "Golden
Gate" long before a
mighty bridge rose
there during the
Great Depression. In
the 1840s, U.S. Army
Captain John C.
Frémont named the
passage Chrysopylae,
or Golden Gate,
because it reminded
him of Istanbul's
Golden Horn Harbor.
The bridge has since
become the interna-
tionally recognized
symbol of San Fran-
cisco. BACK COVER:
Another landmark,
Coit Tower, rose in
1934 on Telegraph
Hill, where a crude
semaphore system
once operated in the
1840s. Coit Tower
memorializes the
city's firefighters.
PAGE 1: Attractive
information kiosks dot
Market Street; many
double as newsstands.
PAGES 2–3: The
Golden Gate Bridge
not only connects
San Francisco with
the Marin headlands
and the rest of
Northern California,
it also joins elements
of the spectacular
Golden Gate National
Recreation Area.

This 1998 edition is published by Crescent Books®,
a division of Random House Value Publishing, Inc.,
201 East 50th Street, New York, N.Y. 10022.

Crescent Books® and colophon are registered trade-
marks of Random House Value Publishing, Inc.

Random House
New York • Toronto • London • Sydney • Auckland
http://www.randomhouse.com/

Printed and bound in China

Library of Congress Cataloging-in-Publication
Data
Highsmith, Carol M., 1946–
San Francisco / Carol M. Highsmith
and Ted Landphair.
p. cm. — (A photographic tour)
Includes index.
ISBN 0-517-20184-4 (hc: alk. paper)
1. San Francisco (Calif.)—Tours.
2. San Francisco (Calif.)—Pictorial works.
I. Landphair, Ted, 1942–   . II. Title. III. Series:
Highsmith, Carol M., 1946–   Photographic tour.
F869.S33H54 1998   97–40006
917.94′610453—dc21   CIP

8   7   6   5   4   3   2   1

Project Editor: Donna Lee Lurker
Designed by Robert L. Wiser, Archetype Press, Inc.,
Washington, D.C.

All photographs by Carol M. Highsmith
unless otherwise credited:
map by XNR Productions, page 5;
painting by Peter Lee Brownlee page 6;
Wells Fargo Historical Services, page 8;
The San Francisco Streetcar Museum, pages 9, 21;
Boudin Baking Company, page 10;
The Library of Congress, Prints &
Photographs Division, pages 11–17, 20;
The Cannery, page 18; The Cliff House, page 19

THE AUTHORS GRATEFULLY ACKNOWLEDGE
THE SUPPORT PROVIDED BY

THRIFTY CAR RENTAL
SAN FRANCISCO
Jim and John Tennant, Owners

HOTEL DIVA

HOTEL GRIFFON

RENOIR HOTEL

IN CONNECTION WITH THE COMPLETION
OF THIS BOOK

THE AUTHORS ALSO WISH TO THANK THE
FOLLOWING FOR THEIR GENEROUS
ASSISTANCE AND HOSPITALITY DURING
THEIR VISITS TO SAN FRANCISCO

San Francisco Convention & Visitors Bureau

American Bistro, Chestnut Street

Maureen Barry

Kristin Rhyan Brown

Helen K. Chang

Merrill R. Cohn

Jean F. DeMouthe

Shirley Fong-Torres

José Godoy

Vera M. Kutschka

Stella Kwiecinski

Charles La Fontaine

Rodney Manson

Marsha Monro

Jon Mulholland

Alain G. Negueloua

Al and Janette Smith, Fresno

Julie Wall

Wesley Williams

Wok Wiz Chinatown Adventure Tours

Ed Ybarrola

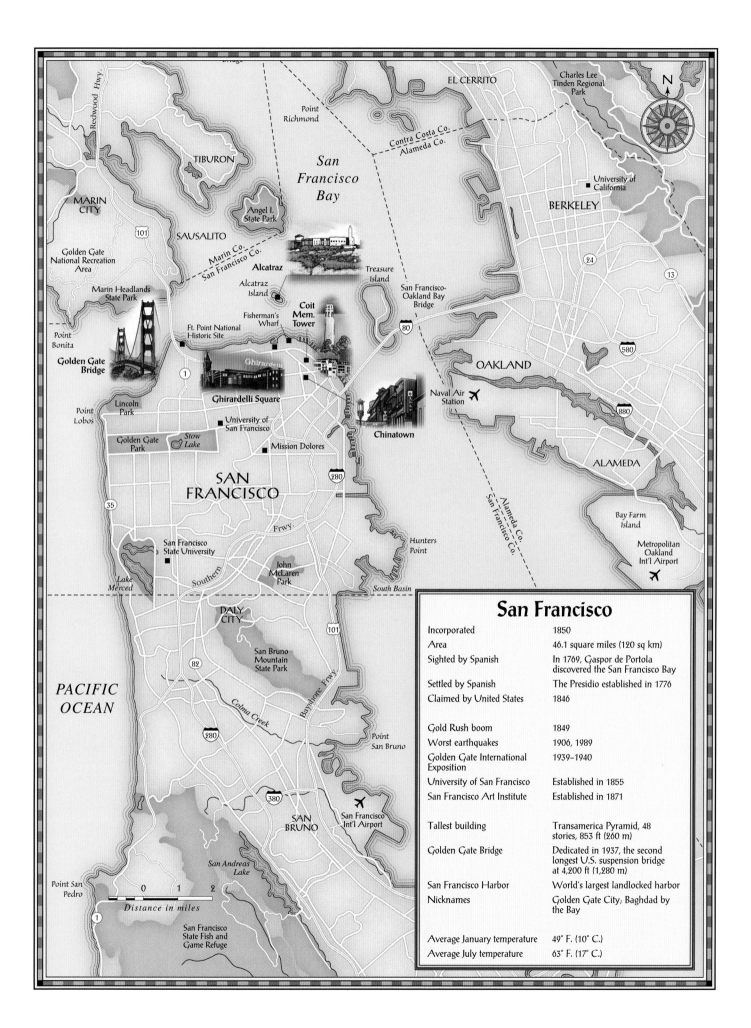

EL CERRITO

Charles Lee
Tinden Regional
Park

N

Point
Richmond

Contra Costa Co.
Alameda Co.

San
Francisco
Bay

University of
California

BERKELEY

TIBURON

MARIN
CITY

Angel I.
State Park

24

SAUSALITO

13

Golden Gate
National Recreation
Area

Marin Co.
San Francisco Co.

Alcatraz

Treasure
Island

Marin Headlands
State Park

Alcatraz
Island

Coit
Mem.
Tower

San Francisco-
Oakland Bay
Bridge

80

580

Point
Bonita

Fisherman's
Wharf

Ft. Point National
Historic Site

OAKLAND

Golden Gate
Bridge

Ghirardelli

1

Ghirardelli Square

Chinatown

Naval Air
Station

880

Point
Lobos

Lincoln
Park

University of
San Francisco

ALAMEDA

Golden Gate
Park

Stow
Lake

Mission Dolores

SAN
FRANCISCO

280

Bay Farm
Island

35

Frwy.

Metropolitan
Oakland
Int'l Airport

San Francisco
State University

Hunters
Point

Alameda Co.
San Francisco Co.

Lake
Merced

Southern

John
McLaren
Park

South Basin

PACIFIC
OCEAN

DALY
CITY

101

San Bruno
Mountain
State Park

82

Bayshore Frwy.

Colma Creek

280

Point
San Bruno

380

San Andreas
Lake

SAN
BRUNO

San Francisco
Int'l Airport

Point San
Pedro

0   1   2

Distance in miles

1

San Francisco
State Fish and
Game Refuge

San Francisco

Incorporated	1850
Area	46.1 square miles (120 sq km)
Sighted by Spanish	In 1769, Gaspor de Portola discovered the San Francisco Bay
Settled by Spanish	The Presidio established in 1776
Claimed by United States	1846
Gold Rush boom	1849
Worst earthquakes	1906, 1989
Golden Gate International Exposition	1939–1940
University of San Francisco	Established in 1855
San Francisco Art Institute	Established in 1871
Tallest building	Transamerica Pyramid, 48 stories, 853 ft (260 m)
Golden Gate Bridge	Dedicated in 1937, the second longest U.S. suspension bridge at 4,200 ft (1,280 m)
San Francisco Harbor	World's largest landlocked harbor
Nicknames	Golden Gate City; Baghdad by the Bay
Average January temperature	49° F. (10° C.)
Average July temperature	63° F. (17° C.)

IN *TRAVELS WITH CHARLEY,* JOHN STEINBECK, THE GREAT AMERICAN novelist, wrote, "San Francisco put on a show for me." And it is still true for the countless visitors to this enchanting "city by the Bay" today. It is hardly uncommon to overhear such exclamations as "Wow! Look at that!" over and over. Such is the beauty of the natural and architectural sights, the geological and meteorological curiosities, and the city's delightful eccentricities. Steinbeck and all those who have spent enough time in San Francisco are well-acquainted with its enticing ambience: the dappled lemon light or the swirling summer fog rolling "like herds of sheep coming to cote in the golden city"; the pelting rain or the multiple rainbows that burst above at once through the streaming sunshine. And there is the city's unique topography of roller-coaster hills and lush green parks, and, of course, the dignified and tightly packed "painted lady" houses, rouged in creams, pinks, and roses. As O. Henry, the famed short-story writer, so scrupulously pointed out: East is East "and West is San Francisco."

While the rest of California sprawls around it, San Francisco is tightly compressed onto a 46.6-square-mile peninsula. Most Californians drive cars that belch exhaust, but San Franciscans whir about on electrified trolleys, motorless cable cars, and gliding BART subway trains. Although every house and every place of business in the twenty or so neighborhoods seems to have one or more cars squeezed in front of it—with wheels angled to the curb to prevent runaways—trucks are a rarity and traffic moves rather briskly. One or two freeways lurk among the city's eucalyptus trees—citizens scuttled another one destined for the Embarcadero—but they use them mainly for jaunts to the airport or a 49ers game or the farms beyond the South Bay. In town, they dash up and down the city's forty-three identifiable hills—two of the hills present a 31.5 percent grade!—on foot or on bicycles, usually without much complaint.

It costs more to live, and certainly to buy a home or rent an apartment, in San Francisco than anywhere else in America. Yet almost no incentive could lure the city's citizens to the suburbs. "It's so livable," San Franciscans say. Behind the Victorian doorways are some of the most creative living arrangements in the nation: opposite and same-sex partnerships, roommate groupings of all descriptions, and fewer nuclear families than in other American cities. Fewer than half the married heterosexual couples in town have children, and schools are relatively lightly populated. Adult San Franciscans seem especially dedicated to careers, avocations, club memberships, entrepreneurship, and cultural affairs.

Per capita, San Francisco has twice as many neighborhood restaurants as New York, and San Franciscans spend more money each year dining out than do residents of any other American city. One can go from high tea to dinner featuring every cuisine from Zairian to ancient Mesopotamian—American chain fast-food joints are rare. They also enjoy a seemingly infinite supply of laundries, corner pubs, coffee and "smoothie" bars, body-piercing parlors, and eclectic art galleries.

By the way, the city should always be called "San Francisco," not "San Fran" or "Frisco," if you want to keep peace with a native. The city and its people are too civilized to accept a nickname. Surprisingly for a Californian city, there are tens of thousands of indigenous San Franciscans to be found, even several generations of them. San Francisco remains the magnet, the crown jewel, the place with "character," although surrounding Bay Area cities have added a museum here, a gallery there, a restaurant row, a glittering new skyscraper, or a hockey team. San Francisco's ballet company, for instance, is the nation's oldest, second-largest, and among the most enthusiastically supported and endowed. Quite simply, San Francisco is "The City" for nearly ten million people from California's Central Valley to the Oregon line.

Renowned, often whimsical, San Francisco and New York artist Peter Lee Brownlee interprets the "crookedest street in the world," the section of Lombard Street that snakes down Russian Hill. This magnet for amateur photographers was too steep for vehicles until zigzag islands decorated with hydrangeas made low-gear auto descents possible.

Uniquely, San Francisco is the nation's most tolerant urban place on one level, and, at the same time, the most hard-headed on another. The city seems to encourage people to "do their own thing," as is evidenced by the robust diversity of racial and sexual pairings, the preponderance of entertainment presentations, streetcorner evangelists, motorcycle menageries, and the gaggles of beggars and sleeping-bag assemblages in the parks. Beginning with its acceptance of homosexuals forced out of the military services during World War II, as well as those who had endured "gay bashings" in other cities around the country, San Francisco—and especially the Castro neighborhood out toward Twin Peaks on Market Street—became universally recognized as the nation's gay capital. It was here that the sewing of the gigantic AIDS memorial quilt sponsored by the NAMES Project—perhaps the largest community art project in the world—began and continues. Estimates of the actual number of openly gay citizens in San Francisco vary, but they have become a powerful, entrenched political and social force here as nowhere else in America. The presence of one hundred thousand or more avowed gay individuals also accounts for the remarkable percentage of single people in San Francisco (approaching 40 percent in most surveys).

The clout and power of another minority group, the Asian community, is also growing strong in San Franciso. Asians outnumber blacks in San Francisco by more than two to one—and Hispanics by the same margin—and many forecasters predict that they will be the city's largest ethnic group by 2020. In many neighborhoods outside Chinatown, Asian banks and restaurants offering "fusion" Asian-American or Asian-European cuisine have started to appear. In addition, Vietnamese and other Southeast Asians have swelled the number of Asians beyond the confines of Chinatown and Japantown.

But San Francisco's fabled tolerance does not always equal permissiveness. After the beatnik craze of the 1950s in North Beach (only in San Francisco could one attend a "Be in"), the Haight neighborhood—around the intersection of Haight and Ashbury streets—in the 1960s became the center of San Francisco hippie "flower power." But the neighborhood was purged of most vagrants and drug dealers when the Haight's "peace and love" devolved into decadence and violence. At one time the city allowed homeless inebriates to congregate in a sanctioned "Wino Park." But in the late 1990s, many San Franciscans began to see them less as society's displaced or disturbed unfortunates than as canny professional panhandlers, and the administration of Mayor Willie Brown started to curb their assembly. Indeed, Brown, like mayors before him, was severely criticized in opinion polls for not doing more to "solve" the homeless problem.

So many interest groups have coalesced—around issues, causes, ethnic groups, and sexual orientations—and grown in political power in San Francisco that any change can trigger paroxysms of protest, even over such minor issues as the closing of a tattered greasy spoon or the removal of a single parking space. For example, in 1971 many San Franciscans mightily opposed, then jeered as unsightly, the 853-foot, pyramidal Transamerica Corporation building that rose on Montgomery Street—the "Wall Street of the West." Of course, that tower—along with the city's cable cars, the Golden Gate Bridge, and Coit Tower—is now one of the most treasured and photographed landmarks in San Francisco. And compromise does not often come

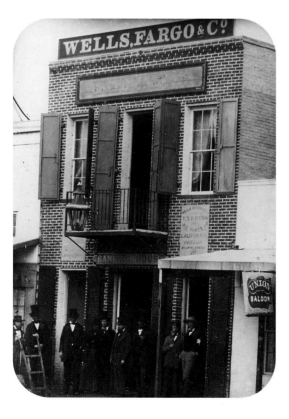

Wells Fargo agencies and stagecoaches were a fixture throughout the West in the late nineteenth century. The company's first banking and express office opened on Montgomery Street in San Francisco in 1852.

smoothly; usually there's a *quid pro quo* involved. For instance, Mayor Dianne Feinstein's administration, in classic San Francisco fashion, underwrote the renovation of an old Norwegian club hall into a headquarters building for the city's many women's groups, but first required that developers of all new office towers agree to set aside funds to construct moderate-income housing somewhere in the city.

A heavily unionized city (even body piercers have a union), San Francisco is accustomed to perennial civic and labor unrest. The people of the city accept this as a tolerable price for its numerous charms: the freshest seafood, sourdough bread, and exotic international cuisines; (nippy) ocean bathing; world-class theater and art, ballet and opera; the lushest landscaped parks west of Philadelphia; two healthy daily newspapers; and everyday vistas that prompt even lifelong San Franciscans to gasp in amazement. In 1997 the *San Francisco Chronicle* extolled the "glory of living anywhere in the Bay Area," where there is always a convenient peak offering a spectacular view. "From the hilltops," gushed the newspaper, "the congestion that makes metropolitan life maddening becomes invisible." From Telegraph, Russian, or Forest Hill, one sees the blue Pacific, the green of a neighborhood park, the khaki hillsides of the Golden Gate National Recreation Area, or the red-rust struts of the Golden Gate Bridge. Not surprisingly, the Mark Hopkins Hotel in San Francisco was the nation's first rooftop barroom that marketed a spectacular city view with the catchphrase: "Watch it get dark at the Top of the Mark." Today, trips up and down one of San Francisco's many glass elevators are among the favorite free "tours" of the city.

San Francisco temperatures, while averaging out to a pleasant sixty degrees or so, can swing wildly with no notice. "The coldest winter I ever spent," goes one refrain, "was a summer in San

This is Kearny Street in 1856—still boomtown days, when buildings seemingly popped up on hillsides overnight. Note the wooden sidewalks. Telegraph Hill, minus today's familiar Coit Tower, is in the distance.

The Boudin family (posing here about 1880 with one of their bakery wagons) delivered their famous sourdough bread throughout San Francisco. The founders of the family-owned bakery, Isidore Boudin and Marie Louise Enri—both French immigrants— married in 1873.

Francisco!" Spared the Santa Ana desert winds that can sizzle Southern California, San Franciscans swelter only in late September and early October's Indian Summer, when the air is mysteriously still and humid. Otherwise, dressing in layers is wise advice, for a toasty day can turn dank and frigid in an instant when the fog rolls in. How foggy does it get, and how often? It's notable that there are twenty-six separate foghorns and other fog signals in the San Francisco Bay alone. In wintertime, waves of rainstorms sometimes roll off the ocean, to be followed by inexplicable periods of climatological perfection.

Perfection? What about the earthquakes? Only tourists ask such questions as natives are calmly stoical on the subject. Their attitude is: "What will be will be." However, that has not stopped them from strengthening the city's buildings or nailing bookcases to the wall, or staying clear of grocery stores and pottery shops when the occasional temblor turns one's footing to jelly. Citizens wearily admit that San Francisco lies within trembling distance of not only the great San Andreas Fault but also several parallel fault lines in the earth's crust. Yes, you'll sway ten feet at the top of a downtown skyscraper during a quake. Yes, the Great Quake of 1906 killed perhaps one thousand people (the actual number is inexact because many undocumented residents were killed in Chinatown) and destroyed nearly every structure east of Van Ness Avenue. But it was the *fires* from ruptured gas mains and fallen lanterns, not tremors or giant cracks in the earth, that produced such horrific loss of life (only by dynamiting a vast firebreak in Van Ness Avenue, destroying great rows of mansions in the process, was the spread of flames arrested). Today's steel reinforcing plus improved fire prevention, as the thinking goes, should prevent such cataclysms again. But what about the Loma Prieta quake in 1989 that flattened part of the San Francisco–Oakland Bay Bridge, darkened the city for days, and sparked fires that consumed much of the Marina

District? More lessons learned, say the natives. And what about the "Big One" that many seismologists believe to be inevitable, perhaps in the foreseeable future? Would downtown skyscraper office space have quadrupled in twenty years if smart money were worried about such things?

What will be will be.

San Francisco long ago gave up trying to compete with Los Angeles or Oakland as a deepwater port, rejecting containerization and the massive wharf space that it would require. Instead it re-created itself as a picturesque tourist enclave of restaurants and shopping meccas in restored warehouses like the Cannery and Ghirardelli (pronounced GEAR-ar-delly) Square. In addition the port services big vessels offshore with tugboat and repair operations, and has ferry operations serving Marin County's upscale Sausalito and Tiburon, Alcatraz Prison, and other Bay Area destinations. Ferries at one time carried fifty million passengers annually from one point to another across the Bay. In its heyday, the great 1898 Ferry Building at the foot of Market Street, with its familiar clock tower and 111 steel-framed concrete piers, was the busiest transportation terminal in America. However, with the opening of the San Francisco–Oakland Bay Bridge in 1936, ferries no longer served as the only link across the Bay. And when the Golden Gate Bridge was finished a year later, a trip up U.S. Highway 101 no longer required a ferry crossing from Fisherman's Wharf to the Marin County shore. The bridge, which can sway more than twenty-five feet in a gale, rise five feet due to expansion on a hot day, and drop ten feet on a cold one, is a triumph of modern engineering—especially considering the swift currents of the two-hundred-foot-deep water below. So popular is the Golden Gate Bridge today that one survey found it was the number-one attraction among foreign visitors to the United States.

In the 1500s, Juan Rodriguez Cabrillo, sailing under the Spanish flag, and Sir Francis Drake, the British explorer, both managed to miss San Francisco Bay as they poked around the California coast—perhaps because of the fog. It would not be until 1769 that the first Spanish galleon sailed into the bay that John C. Frémont would later call "the Golden Gate." Seven years later the first Spanish colonists arrived from Mexico. They established a *presidio* (fort), a mission (one in a string of twenty-one along *El Camino Real*—the Royal Highway—from San Diego to Sonoma), and a pueblo. The missions were established by Franciscan monks intent on converting "pagan" Indian souls. The peaceful, agrarian Ohlones were quickly subjugated and put to work as gardeners and weavers. Notwithstanding, they were annihilated by the pestilant diseases of the white man against which they had no immunity.

Not until Mexico gained control of California many years later did the settlement get a name, Yerba Buena ("Good Herb")—not San Francisco, honoring the Franciscans' founder and already the name of the vast bay that bordered the peninsula. The Spanish paid the place little mind save to keep a wary eye on the Russians, who had established a thriving trading post sixty miles north at Fort Ross, from which they hunted seals and sea otters. Besides, the land surrounding Yerba Buena was largely covered with sand, including gigantic dunes stretching six miles from the ocean, clear across the peninsula.

By the time Mexico lost California to the United States in 1848, following a brief and disastrous war over Texas, Americans had already settled much of Northern California. In 1846 they even seized Sonoma, north of San Francisco, briefly establishing a fragile republic and

Streetcars (not cable cars) rumbled near Douglas Tilden's monument marking California's 1850 admission to the Union. The statue was unveiled at the intersection of Market, Mason, and Turk streets in 1897, but was later moved.

hoisting a flag bearing the likeness of a grizzly bear. That same year, Captain John Berrein Montgomery sailed the USS *Portsmouth* into Yerba Buena harbor and raised the American flag with nary a shot fired in resistance. According to one of his crew who chronicled the moment, "Capt. M had a proclamation all ready prepared and our first Lieutenant now read it to the assembled crowd and when he finished gave the signal, and in a moment, amid the roar of cannon from the ship, and hurrahs of the ship's company, the vivas of the Californians, the cheers of the Dutchmen, the barking of dogs, braying of jackasses and a general confusion of sounds from every living thing within hearing, that flag floated up, which has never been lowered to mortal foe." Portsmouth Square, now on the edge of Chinatown, marks the spot of this "conquest" of San Francisco—two years before the rest of California formally became American.

Golden Gate Park, which rose atop sandy wasteland, was a favorite strolling ground in the late nineteenth century. The Conservatory of Flowers, originally identical to the greenhouse at London's Kew Gardens, was later expanded.

Within a few months of Montgomery's arrival, Yerba Buena had a mayor—Washington A. Bartlett—and acquired a couple hundred new residents. They were Mormons who had sailed from New York in hopes of joining Brigham Young, who had marched westward from Illinois in search of a new Promised Land for his Latter-Day Saints. (Young and his followers, of course, stopped and stayed at Utah's Great Salt Lake.) Sam Brannan, one of the town's new Mormons, started a newspaper, which soon opposed Bartlett's first sweeping directive, changing the name of the town to match the better-known name for the surrounding Bay. But Bartlett won the day. "San Francisco" it would be.

San Francisco became a port of moderate importance with about five hundred souls, and 150 buildings and tents. But in 1848, James Marshall, a sawmill operator, found gold on a farm owned by John Sutter more than a hundred miles away in the foothills of the Sierra Mountains.

The discovery quickly ended the city's days as a muddy shantytown, where one downtown corner was marked with a sign reading, "This street impassable, not even jackassable." Gold fever, too, quickly roused interest in full-fledged statehood for California. After vigorous debate over whether the territory should enter the Union as a free or slave-holding state, California was admitted as a free state in 1850. A year earlier, eighty thousand prospectors—"Forty-Niners" for whom the football team is named—had descended on San Francisco en route to the hills. In the two years that followed, one-hundred-twenty thousand more Americans left their homes in search of El Dorado, making the arduous journey across the continent, by ship around Cape Horn, or over the swampy Isthmus of Panama and then by ship to San Francisco. Ironically both Sutter, the owner of the mill on which gold had been discovered, and Marshall, the discoverer, would die penniless after the frenzied Forty-Niners overran the goldfield.

San Franciscans delighted in their Sutro Baths, which at one time was the world's largest bath-house. Located below the spectacular Cliff House at Point Lobos, it housed six salt baths and hundreds of dressing rooms. Here, frolickers enjoy "The Shoot" water slide in 1898.

Though not a nugget of gold was ever unearthed in San Francisco, it was the city by the Bay—not the Sierra boomtowns near the Mother Lode—that was transformed into the true City of Gold. San Francisco supplied the transportation, foodstuffs, clothing—including Levi Strauss's blue-denim work pants with copper buttons and rivets—tools, whiskey, bawdy entertainers, and financing that fueled the boom. At first, though, San Francisco itself was almost emptied as every other neighbor seemed to have headed east in search of fortune. Much of the wealth from the goldfields ended up in San Francisco—in its wharves and hotels, clothing stores and banks. Even established Americans heroes like William Tecumseh Sherman—as a prominent banker—moved to San Francisco to get in on the action. These were raucous times, during which the city's abidance of singular characters and unconventional lifestyles was most likely born.

Notable among the lovable crackpots was "Emperor" Joshua Norton, a failed commodities speculator from South Africa who, after proclaiming himself "Emperor of the United States and Protector of Mexico," printed his own promissory notes and set off across San Francisco in search of free meals. The populace found this harebrain who dressed in a top hat and epauletted uniform so endearing that establishments were all too happy to oblige. Tom Cole, in his delightful *Short History of San Francisco*, reports that "when Emperor Norton died in 1880—just as his countless promissory notes were coming due, he was given a teary municipal funeral (paid for by the swells of the Pacific Club, later the Pacific Union, then and now the city's most exclusive men's club). Ten thousand people passed by his coffin and a boy's choir sang 'Nearer My God to Thee.'" According to Cole, even today, iconoclastic San Franciscans will occasionally gin up a "Norton festival," just for old times' sake.

In the wake of the gold stampede, the city's waterfront at the end of Pacific Avenue became a slatternly Murderer's Row of bars and brothels, terrorized by gangs—including some comprised of British thugs called "Sydney Ducks" who had somehow escaped their banishment to Australia. It was called "the Barbary Coast" in a grudging nod to the pirate-infested states of North Africa. B. E. Lloyd described the San Francisco version as a pit of "licentiousness, debauchery, pollution, loathsome disease, insanity from dissipation, misery, poverty, wealth, profanity, blasphemy and death." He said the docks were a Hell "yawning to receive the putrid mass." Vigilante committees, led by the righteous Sam Brannan and others, finally became fed

In 1900, Chinatown residents scan news reports of the Boxer Rebellion, an effort by a Chinese secret society to end foreign influence in China. In those days, intrigue and gang warfare also marked life in San Francisco's Chinatown.

up and hanged a few malefactors, cleared the vice dens, and ran many out of town. In due time—following a series of disastrous fires that helped clean out the most wretched neighborhoods—an orderly Embarcadero boulevard was laid out from the Barbary Coast and beyond, out to Fisherman's Wharf. During one of those fires a little girl, Lillie Coit, was saved by the Knickerbocker Engine Co. No. 5, based near Telegraph Hill. She thereafter tagged along everywhere the fire brigade went. Wealthy and eccentric later in life (often dressing as a man in order to join in poker games), she bequeathed $100,000 to honor the city's firefighters. The city built Coit Tower with the money. It is now a landmark atop Telegraph Hill. According to local lore, just as often debunked, the tower resembles a fireman's nozzle.

Just as the city was retrenching, stratifying, and settling into orderly ways, San Francisco sprang to life as a boomtown a second time when a great lode of silver that was discovered in "them thar hills." Men like Henry Comstock (of the "Comstock Lode") and James "Old Virginny" Finney (of "Virginia City")—not to mention chroniclers like Mark Twain who wrote about them—spread silver fever worldwide and cemented San Francisco's position as the financial and mercantile hub of the swaggering New West. Embodying the braggadocio of the times was the construction of the Palace, the world's largest hotel, built in 1875 for five million dollars by city pioneers William Sharon and William Chapman Ralston. It later hosted President Warren G. Harding and King David Kalakaua of Hawaii—both of whom died in the hotel.

Another landmark of the Gilded Age was the Cliff House, an eight-story grand chateau that loomed precariously on a bluff overlooking the Pacific at Ocean Beach. It was actually the second incarnation of what was originally a smaller, unseemly gambling hall and bordello that burned to the ground. Tycoon Adolph Sutro, who made his fortune building a tunnel through Nevada's Sun Mountain to the Comstock Lode, rebuilt the Cliff House and turned it into the city's favorite resort. A promenade to the Cliff House for Sunday brunch was a requisite ritual for local families and their out-of-town guests, as was a splash in the "Sutro Baths" below his nearby estate. There, for fifty cents, patrons could rent a towel, locker, and long woolen swim suit; splash in any of seven saltwater pools of varying temperatures; and frolic on any of seven slides or thirty rings suspended above the pools. The second Cliff House miraculously survived the Great Quake of '06, only to burn down a year later. The baths—and a delightful amusement arcade on the beach—lasted well into the century, closing only after television and other distractions eroded their popularity. A third Cliff House, designed by the architects of the Fairmont Hotel and modeled more closely on the first structure than the second, opened in 1909; the National Park Service took over the entire site in 1977.

It was a self-confident, new world-class city that could afford to create Golden Gate Park, a giant horticultural showcase, atop the sand dunes in the far-western reaches of town. Landscape architect William Hammond Hall, a twenty-four-year-old disciple of Frederick Law Olmsted, figured out ways to cover the existing dunes with plantings and stop the onslaught of sand off Ocean Beach by building a giant seawall. By adding wells and two windmills, Hall brought one more vital ingredient to the equation: water, which turned the park green. In 1894, Golden Gate Park was the site of the first of three great San Francisco world's fairs, three remnants of which—a grand Japanese tea garden, a music concourse, and the classic De Young art museum—remain among the statuary, arboretums, and conservatories in this remarkable piece of urban landscaping.

All the while, San Francisco was coming to grips with its first widespread incidents of racial intolerance against the city's large Chinese population. Almost fifty thousand Chinese were brought to the United States from Canton and the surrounding Kwangtung Province as cheap labor for the gold camps and the great transcontinental railroad stretching east from Sacramento. They were settled into a crowded quarter where their industriousness brought them prominence in the garment industry and other enterprises. But in the late 1870s, when bank failures and a depression tied to overspeculation spread unemployment across the city, many white San Franciscans blamed the Chinese. Suspicion was fueled by tales—not all of them exaggerated—of opium dens, "tong" wars, sweatshops, and trafficking in slave girls. Such intrigue made Chinatown then, like the much more respectable Chinese quarter today, a favored city tourist attraction. But it was angry mobs, not tourists, who twice stormed into Chinatown, burning and beating as they went.

It was during the last quarter of the nineteenth century that most of the city's treasured Victorian houses were built. Made of redwood and laden with gingerbread trim, fourteen thousand homes were constructed, costing from $1,000 to $5,000 each to build. They were exuberantly painted and came in five distinct styles—including "San Francisco Stick"—cobbled from patterns seen in magazines and architectural books. Affordable housing was essential for the city to accommodate growth and expansion. Seen today as symbols of economic comfort, achievement, and individuality, the rows of Victorians that spread up the

This is the second, and most magnificent, Cliff House built above Ocean Beach and the popular Playland amusement park. In 1902, seemly citizens sample the sea air but disdain the breaking waves.

The Great Quake of 1906—and the more destructive fires that it triggered—left little standing in the eastern half of the city. Unreinforced masonry structures crumbled, and wooden buildings were easily consumed by fire.

city's steep hills and out toward Golden Gate Park were at the time, ironically, disdained for their *un*imaginativeness.

Mobility around the city was greatly enhanced with the development of the cable car—the ingenious invention of Andrew Hallidie, who was already making cable for use in the mines. After he successfully demonstrated that streetcars might traverse the city's hills by simply grabbing on to an endlessly moving cable running beneath the street in 1873, eight separate cable-car companies sprang up, and the idea was copied in cities from Sydney to Washington.

Not just the middle class benefited from the cable cars, electric trolleys, and automobiles that gave San Franciscans mastery over their hills. So did the wealthy who built mansions on Nob Hill and financed housing developments in the streetcar suburb called the "Western Addition" and elsewhere. Among the "Big Four" wealthiest of the wealthy was Leland Stanford—another Central Pacific mogul—who created the great university near Palo Alto in memory of a son.

These were the days when San Francisco was by far the dominant city of the West Coast—Los Angeles at the time was little more than a sleepy citrus center—and it attracted not only the rich, but also some of the nation's most audacious writers and editors. Among them were some of America's famous fiction writers: Mark Twain, Bret Harte (who romanticized the Gold Rush), and Jack London. Newspaper tycoon William Randolph Hearst perfected his brand of muckraking "yellow journalism" at the *San Francisco Examiner,* which his father, George, a silver baron from the Comstock Lode days, had given him as a present. Later in the twentieth century in the "beatnik" days of the 1950s and the psychedelic era of 1960s, counterculture writers like Jack Kerouac, Ken Kesey, and Allen Ginsberg flourished here.

Entire tent cities sprang up in all the city's parks immediately after the devastating '06 Quake. Businesses moved their entire operations to the park. Someone titled this photograph, "Making the Best of It."

The early years of the twentieth century in San Francisco were marked by the explosive growth of unions, built upon resentment of the city's capitalist elite. Strikes, rioting, wild newspaper wars, and waves of reform swept the city. Then came the terrifying '06 Quake that would destroy four-fifths of the city and leave an estimated 250,000 residents homeless. "City practically ruined by fire," read the last message coming from the city's main telegraph office nine hours after the quake. "No water. It's awful. There is no communication anywhere and entire phone system busted. I want to get out of here or be blown up." In the days that followed, clean-up crews, tent cities, and relief kitchens spread across the city, and within three years thousands of homes and businesses were rebuilt. Even before the Great Quake and fire, city leaders had endorsed a "City Beautiful" campaign, inspired by architect Daniel Burnham's "Great White City" plan for Chicago's 1893 World's Columbian Exposition. Burnham himself was invited to create a master plan for San Francisco, full of alabaster buildings, wide boulevards, bucolic parks, and hilltop aeries. The rush to rebuild the city scrapped much of Burnham's plan, though developers paid him a passing nod in their blueprints for the reclaimed city. As a symbol of its rebirth, San Francisco's flag features a phoenix rising from the ashes.

In 1912, voters approved a bond issue to finance an entire neoclassical Civic Center, including a new City Hall, an opera house, a civic auditorium, and a grand public library. City Hall was completed in 1915, the year San Francisco announced its recovery to the world with the shining Panama-Pacific International Exposition near the Presidio. The Exposition celebrated the completion of the Panama Canal—a boon to California commerce—and was dominated by a glittering (and temporary) "Tower of Jewels" and Palace of Fine Arts.

More strikes, notably among longshoremen and supportive Teamsters Union drivers coupled

After Del Monte Company male workers delivered lugs of peaches to preparation tables in the building now called the Cannery, women cut each peach in half and removed the pits with spoon-shaped knives.

with the financial blows of the Great Depression further staggered "the Wall Street of the West." On "Bloody Thursday," July 5, 1934, more than one hundred men were injured and two killed in fighting at picket lines at Pier 38. A citywide strike followed, closing theaters, restaurants, and even liquor stores. The result was nearly total capitulation by employers, the recognition of unions and most of their demands, and the solidification of San Francisco as the nation's most solidly unionized town.

Paradoxically, it was also during this period of upheaval in which the great Golden Gate and Bay bridges, and Coit Tower, were built, and Alcatraz Island—long a military prison—was turned over to the Federal Government to house the "worst of the worst" federal prisoners. Such infamous criminals as Al ("Scarface") Capone, George ("Baby Face") Nelson, George ("Machine Gun") Kelly, Alvin ("Creepy") Karpis, and Robert Stroud were among the new inmates. Stroud, later made famous by the movie *The Birdman of Alcatraz* starring Burt Lancaster, never kept a bird on the island; it was specifically to get rid of his aviary and special treatment that officials had him moved from Leavenworth Prison, where his nickname had been "The Bird Doctor of Leavenworth."

These were the years, too, of the Golden Gate International Exposition, San Francisco's third great world's fair, staged on a manmade island next to the new San Francisco–Oakland Bay Bridge. "Treasure Island," the locals took to calling it, for it featured a giant Arch of Triumph, a "Court of the Moon," and a "Tower of the Sun." The 1939–40 fair featured great shows, including an "Aquacade" starring Johnny Weissmuller and Esther Williams. A year later, when the Japanese attacked Pearl Harbor near Honolulu, the Navy turned Treasure Island into a naval training and embarkation center and airstrip. San Francisco girded for war and braced for a Japanese attack that never came by stringing antisubmarine netting across the Golden Gate and building gun batteries all around the Bay. But it prospered as only once before—during the Gold Rush—as shipyards sprang to life and wartime goods by the millions poured out of San Francisco harbor.

The years since World War II have solidified San Francisco's reputation as a cultured, comely, and occasionally kooky place. The beatniks were followed, in the 1960s, by the New Left protesters—centered, actually, across the Bay in Berkeley—the hippies, and the psychedelic "San Francisco Sound" rock groups like the Grateful Dead, the Jefferson Airplane, and Quicksilver Messenger Service. Writer Joan Didion wrote that San Francisco was the flashpoint of the nation's "social hemorrhaging" during the hippie years. Then in 1978 came citywide disquiet following the assassination of Mayor George Moscone and Harvey Milk, the first openly gay supervisor, by Dan White, a disgruntled former supervisor. White and Milk seemed to embody the fractiousness of San Francisco politics, as each represented a different ward and vocal constituency. William Saroyan once described San Francisco as "an experiment in living," and that observation still rings true in the 1990s as the city continues to be a source of endless fascination.

The spirit of experimentation, a part of the city's character from the raucous days of the Gold Rush, is reflected throughout the city in its people as well as its civic life, transportation, arts, and architecture. One just has to look at the city's unique collection of soaring skyscrapers in the Financial District, which includes the four massive towers of Embarcadero Center, the cross-braced Alcoa Building, and the Bank of America Center. The most distinct is the great Transamerica Pyramid. It is unusual in its own right and made ever more distinctive by its odd geometric supports called "isosceles tetrahedrons" at its base. They are not merely decorative as they provide shock absorber-type protection in earthquakes. And few visitors ever realize that the entire Financial District was built upon a landfill covering an old cove of San Francisco Bay, and that this area, spreading into North Beach, was once the infamous Barbary Coast.

Not far away is Union Square, the city's chic shopping district, ringed by fine hotels and high-end clothing and department stores. Union Square was once one of the few open spaces in the city's crowded center. It was given to the city by John Geary, the first elected mayor of the newly chartered (1850) city of San Francisco, and got its name when Union sympathizers rallied there during the Civil War. Just down Geary Street is the theater district, packed with charming little hotels and art galleries. A few blocks away is Chinatown—the world's largest Chinese community outside Asia—still mostly confined to the forty-two blocks where it originated. With its herbal pharmacies, curio shops, hundreds of restaurants and dim-sum parlors, fruit and poultry markets, walk-in temples, and narrow alleys, Chinatown remains a delightful curiosity. Less sinister—and less fragrant—than a century ago, Chinatown still excites the senses. A one-mile-square Japantown ginza is farther out at Post and Geary streets; there, a giant plaza is surrounded by enchanting little gardens lined with bonsai trees.

North Beach, out on Grant Street toward the Bay, has lost some of its Italian flavor from the days when sailors, longshoremen, and their families lived, shopped, and cooked pasta here. But it's still quaint and tightly packed, the home of kitschy theaters, jazz and comedy clubs, and, still, some of the finest little Italian restaurants in the country. Not far away, at Fisherman's

San Francisco City Hall, completed in 1915, was the centerpiece of the magnificent new Civic Center. Architects rank it along with the museums surrounding the Washington Mall as triumphs of the "City Beautiful" movement.

Wharf and its surrounding piers, the smells of fresh-cooked crabs, hot sourdough bread, giant shrimps en cocktail, and chocolates from Ghirardelli Square swirl irresistibly, as do the spices, cheeses, and sausages in the old Del Monte canning factory that's now the Cannery shopping gallery. This is also the departure point, via ferry connections, to other exotic places: Sausalito's artist colony, a creepy tour of Alcatraz, and an inspiring walk through the redwoods of Muir Woods. Down the hill from Ghirardelli Square is the National Maritime Museum, a reminder of the city's seafaring history.

San Francisco's marina, out toward the Golden Gate along the waterfront, is smaller than expected but fully intoxicating. It is also the gateway to the majestic Palace of Fine Arts and the 1,480-acre Presidio, the old U.S. Army base. Originally Spanish and now one of America's newest national parks, it is as trim and well maintained as it was in the days when the Sixth Army guarded the entrance to San Francisco Bay. Hidden on the Presidio grounds are the city's largest forest, a great national cemetery, a fine army museum, and even a whimsical pet cemetery—once reserved for military beasts like General John J. Pershing's horse, but now filled with tributes to assorted parakeets, Chihuahuas, and kitty-cats. This area is also the beginning of the Golden Gate National Recreation Area, the world's largest urban park and the most-visited national park in America, which spreads across the Bay to Marin County and the remote Point Reyes Peninsula.

Ocean Beach and Golden Gate Park are not part of this recreation area, but they might as well be, for they attract thousands of San Franciscans out for a cool, leisurely departure from their daily lives. Ocean Beach lures surfers and hang-gliders as well as bathers looking for a bracing splash in the sea, and photographers looking to capture Seal Rocks beyond the Cliff House. A drive through Golden Gate Park alone is refreshing, not even counting stops at the many attractions within the park: the Asian and De Young art museums; the Smithsonian-caliber California Academy of Sciences; the enchanting Conservatory of Flowers, the Shakespeare Garden, and the Japanese Tea Garden; and one of two Dutch-style windmills that once drew water to saturate the park.

Until the opening of New York's Verrazano-Narrows Bridge in 1964, the Golden Gate Bridge at 1.7 miles was the world's longest single span. More notoriously, the bridge claimed eleven lives during its construction and has been the site of nearly one thousand suicides.

The Panhandle, a tiny protruberence of Golden Gate Park, extends eastward into the Haight-Ashbury section—once an area of peaceful dairy farms—and now an eclectic neighborhood of "painted ladies" and stubborn counterculturists. To this day, tour buses ply Haight Street in search of "freaks," and suburban parents drop their kids for a day of cruising "head shops" and second-hand clothing stores, while an occasional lost soul can be spotted pushing a hand mower toward Panhandle Park, muttering, "I'm going to the park to cut some *grass,* man." Despite the remaining vestiges of 1960s counterculture, "the Haight" has become a model of gentrification. There's even a chain ice-cream store on one corner of Haight and Ashbury, and a chain clothier on another.

Above the Haight are some of the city's most vibrant and prestigious small neighborhoods, including Pacific Heights, Inner and Outer Richmond, and Upper Fillmore. With the University of San Francisco's main campus nearby, streets like Chestnut, Geary, and Sacramento teem with student activity at bookstores, coffee shops, and movie theaters. The area's delightful little restaurants bring in traffic from throughout the city. Around Alamo Square are classic Victorian homes like the opulent 1886 Haas-Lilienthal House and the "Postcard Row"

of houses so often photographed against the skyline of downtown high rises. Closer to downtown are Nob Hill—ever the elite address—as well as the less ritzy environs of the Tenderloin, the location of the city's underbelly of soup kitchens, nudie shows, and police substations that is ever-so-slowly being upgraded.

Market Street, which plunges southwest from the Financial District and the Tenderloin past the Civic Center to the Castro neighborhood in Eureka Valley, is a familiar dividing line. It is sometimes maddening for the visitor to cross as some streets make it through, others dead-end, and most are one-way. The neighborhoods below Market, including one actually called "South of Market"—or "SoMa"—are less expensive and less haughty than those above Market. Walkers note: the blocks south of Market are larger, too—roughly four times as large—which helps explain why much of the area was consigned to light industry. The city's Museum of Modern Art and the graceful Yerba Buena Gardens across the street as well as the sprawling Moscone Convention Center were built here. Toward Mission Street south of Market, too, is the city's Hispanic heartland—the Mission District—built around the 1791 Mission Dolores and now dotted with colorful grocery stores, flower shops, and exuberant murals.

If such a thing could possibly be measured, San Francisco might well be the world's favorite city. Despite its compactness, no visit seems to cover it all. When one must leave, it's with the feeling of privilege at having met this unforgettable *grande dame*. Suave yet naughty, winsome yet brawling, seagazing as well as seagoing, courtly yet avant garde, San Francisco seizes the senses. Tony Bennett, the great crooner, in his famous rendition of the song about this city, left his heart here. It's little wonder, for San Francisco is a siren, whose song once heard is never forgotten.

Haight Street in 1944 bore little resemblance to the hippie haven that it would become two decades later. Alcohol, readily available all along the street, was then the neighborhood's drug of choice.

OVERLEAF: San Francisco's hills are not so noticeable at night when lights commingle into a galaxy-like display. Earthquake-resistant steel frame construction, with pilings sunk to bedrock, made high-rise construction possible.

Market Street (above), leading straight downtown, has been a dividing line between dense development to the north and less congestion to the south. Because of its affordability, developers of "SoMa," or South of Market, have been increasingly active here. The 1972 Transamerica Pyramid (opposite), San Francisco's tallest building, with its windowless "wings"—viewed here from an observation deck at the Mandarin Oriental Hotel—rises forty-eight stories, in addition to a 212-foot tower. Architect William Pereira chose the pyramidal configuration to bring more light to street level than a conventional boxy skyscraper would have allowed. The tower is part of a block-long complex that includes lush Redwood Park and an outdoor performing stage. Embarcadero Center (overleaf) has been called a city within a city. This massive shopping, office, and hotel complex was built in stages over fourteen years, beginning in 1967. Its four towers are linked by footbridges.

Ralph Stackpole's cast-stone sculptures (opposite) loom beside the entrance to the temple-like Pacific Stock Exchange Building. The exchange had planned to locate elsewhere in 1930, but the Stock Market crash of 1929 prompted the less costly renovation of a vacated 1915 U.S. Treasury building. The Wells Fargo Bank branch office (top left) at Market and Grant streets dates from 1910, when it was built by the Union Trust Bank. The banks merged in 1923. A popular exhibit at the Wells Fargo History Museum on Montgomery Street is an 1868 Concord stagecoach (bottom left), the backbone of the company's express service. Remarkably, these coaches carried as many as eighteen people, in addition to luggage. The museum interprets the history of the entire West.

The opulent Garden Court (left), originally a carriage courtyard, of the Sheraton Palace Hotel is one of the world's most beautiful dining rooms. The Palace epitomized the swagger of the New West. Built in 1875 by pioneers William Sharon and William Chapman Ralston, it survived the Great '06 earthquake, only to burn to the ground after firefighters drained its four artesian wells and 630,000-gallon reservoir. One of the world's most sophisticated hotel bars is the Clift Hotel's Redwood Room (above). Its walls and columns were crafted in 1934 from the wood of a single giant sequoia redwood tree that had been felled by lightning.

The Tadich Grill (opposite), San Francisco's oldest restaurant, opened in 1849 during the Gold Rush. Restaurateur/designer Pat Kuleto created a stir in 1997 when he opened Farallon restaurant (left), with its upscale "coastal cuisine" and $4-million undersea-fantasy decor—including custom-made "jellyfish" sculpted lights and a "nautilus room" worthy of Jules Verne. San Francisco's endearing Brown Twins—Marian, left, and Vivian—enjoy afternoon tea at one of San Francisco's most popular rendezvous spots: the Westin St. Francis Hotel's Compass Rose Room (above). The twins are fixtures in advertisements as far away as Germany. Union Square (overleaf) is the heart of the city's shopping and hotel district. Winged Victory stands atop the square's monument, dedicated to Spanish-American War hero Admiral George Dewey in 1903.

The Tenderloin District, between downtown and the Civic Center, has long been San Francisco's sleazy Skid Row, full of soup kitchens, bawdy theaters (above), flophouses, and massage parlors. Rents are cheap, so the district has also had a high concentration of respectable older residents. The area has been improving slowly thanks to beefed-up police presence, an influx of Southeast Asian immigrants, and the determined renovations of some of the area's hotels and businesses. The acclaimed American Conservatory Theater repertory company's showcase is the Geary Theater (right) in the heart of the Theater District off Union Square. The 1909 Geary building abuts another noted Classical-style theater hall, built in 1922, that houses the Curran Theatre. There are also other exceptional legitimate theaters elsewhere in town.

San Francisco's magnificent War Memorial Opera House (above), designed by G. Albert Lansburgh, was modeled after Garnier's Paris Opera. Renovated in the 1990s after sustaining earthquake damage, the auditorium is a centerpiece of the Baroque Revival–style Civic Center that also includes City Hall. Principal dancer Yuri Possokhov and soloist Julie Diana from the nonpareil San Francisco Ballet (opposite) limber up in the auditorium's resplendent lobby. The nation's oldest and second-largest ballet company, the San Francisco Ballet first performed in the new Opera House in 1933. The company presented the first full-length American production of Swan Lake in 1939 and launched a nationwide holiday tradition when it first performed the Nutcracker in 1944. Yerba Buena Gardens (overleaf), built atop Moscone Convention Center facilities, offer a sparkling view of downtown, including the truncated cylindrical skylight of the San Francisco Museum of Modern Art.

"It is hard to tell which has shaped the other more
What does matter is that the mutuality was import

The Friends of Photography, a membership-supported arts organization, operates the Ansel Adams Center for Photography (above) in the Yerba Buena Gardens redevelopment area. It showcases the work of several photographers, including Adams, the pioneer wilderness photographer. He was heavily involved in the Sierra Club, and its image came to be defined by Adams's photographs. "I believe the approach of the artist and the approach of the environmentalist are fairly close," Adams once said, "in that both are, to a rather impressive degree, concerned with the 'affirmation of life.'" Dedicated in 1995, the San Francisco Museum of Modern Art (opposite), designed by Swiss architect Mario Botta in association with San Francisco's HOK firm, includes fifty thousand square feet of gallery space, almost doubling the exhibition space of its old Civic Center location. Its atrium opens onto studio spaces, a bookstore, and a café.

More than 170 ferries
once docked at the
impressive Ferry
Building (above)
below Market Street.
Built by state engi-
neers beginning in
1895, the terminal
was converted to office
use after most ferries
stopped running in
the 1950s. The double-
deck San Francisco–
Oakland Bay Bridge
(right), which opened
in 1936, reaches the
East Bay in two stages,
meeting at Yerba
Buena Island midway
across the Bay. One
upper end section of
the bridge collapsed
onto the lower level
during the fearsome
1989 Loma Prieta
earthquake. Amaz-
ingly, only one person
died, and the bridge
was reinforced
and reopened in
one month. Along
the Embarcadero,
the lampposts of
Herb Caen Way
(overleaf)—named
for the late, beloved
San Francisco Chron-
icle columnist—set
a moody foreground
for the bridge.

The USS Jeremiah O'Brien *(left), berthed at Pier 32, was a "Liberty Ship" that carried grain, troops, and armaments to European and Pacific outposts during World War II. The ship is not mothballed; the crew still occasionally runs her out into the Bay. The* Jeremiah *is open for tours, and the engines are occasionally fired for visitors. Red's Java House (above) has long been a favorite stop for longshoremen and other blue-collar workers like retired heavy-equipment operator Mazzini Maffioli and his son Mike, a courier. No one is quite sure how far back the tiny breakfast and sandwich joint dates, but its customers consider the shack historic enough that they have successfully blocked attempts to demolish or move the hash house for urban redevelopment.*

Redwood
Bank

In the 1970s, Hollywood producer Francis Ford Coppola bought, remodeled, and established his American Zoetrope production studios in the flatiron Columbus Tower (opposite, foreground)—also called the Sentinel Building—in North Beach. It had just opened when the devastating 1906 earthquake struck and was one of the few downtown structures to survive. The corrupt Abe Ruef, an unelected power broker, once ran the city from this building. In North Beach, too, is the intimate Club Fugazi, home of Beach Blanket Babylon, the nation's longest-running musical revue—so long-running that an entire section of Green Street has been renamed "Beach Blanket Babylon Boulevard." Chanteuse Val Diamond (above) models one of the outrageously outsized hats for which the production is famous. The show is based loosely on Snow White's worldwide quest for her prince. Nearby Chinatown (overleaf) is one of the city's oldest and most densely populated neighborhoods.

The Bank of Canton is located in a building (opposite) that once housed a telephone exchange. Completed in 1909—three years after the Great Quake destroyed most of Chinatown—this pagoda was the first Chinese-style structure built in the city. Cantonese, rather than China's official Mandarin dialect, is the first language in much of Chinatown; the neighborhood's first residents were imported as mine and railroad workers from Canton and the surrounding province. Telephone exchange operators had to know five dialects and memorize the numbers of all of their customers. Callers would ask for their parties by name. Exotic shops and trading companies (left) still dot Chinatown, which has been reformed and modernized since the days when sinister gangs prowled and opium dens operated in the rear of several restaurants.

The Ma-Tsu (Heavenly Mother) Temple of the U.S.A. (above) is open for prayer and scripture readings, community meetings, and even exercise classes. The temple, which opened in 1986, is a branch of the Ma-Tsu Temple in Taiwan. Executive Chef Howard Wong (opposite) perfects "haute cuisine Chinoise" at Tommy Toy's, one of the city's most elegant restaurants, which is not in Chinatown but on Montgomery Street in the city's Financial District. Wong's dishes combine French and Chinese delicacies. (Toy calls the fare Frenchinoise.) Compact San Francisco—it squeezes into less than 47 square miles—has more than thirty-three hundred restaurants. The city's food is so acclaimed that several of the city's tours include dinner in their packages. A survey in the late 1990s showed that San Franciscans themselves eat out more than do residents of any other large American city.

56

GRACE CATHEDRAL

After the mansion belonging to Comstock Lode millionaire Charles Crocker burned in the Great Quake of 1906, his family gave the Nob Hill property to the Episcopal diocese. Architect Lewis Hobart was commissioned to design a cathedral for the site. Grace Cathedral (left) was built in several stages beginning in 1928. It was not fully completed until 1964. Although the exterior resembles stone, it was made of reinforced concrete because of seismic considerations; the concrete was then brushed to give it the appearance of stone. The main doors (above), installed in 1964, were copied from Lorenzo Ghiberti's bronze Gates of Paradise *from the* Cathedral Bapistry in Florence. The sounds of Grace Cathedral's carillon, as well as its pipe organ, resound across midtown, especially during the Christmas season.

59

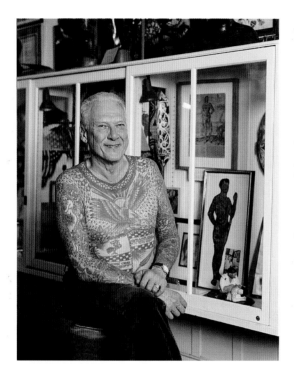

Lyle Tuttle (above) once ran San Francisco's only tattoo parlor. Now there are dozens, many doubling as body-piercing emporiums. Tuttle—whose clients have included celebrities like Joan Baez, Janis Joplin, and Cher—has turned his studio into the Tattoo Art Museum. Incidentally, that is not a shirt that he's wearing. Victor Amauloff executed the fresco mural (right), one of several decorating Coit Tower's interior walls. The murals were commissioned by the federal government in the 1930s as a public-works project depicting life in California. In The Pedestrian Scene, note the holdup taking place, unnoticed by the passersby. Cable cars (overleaf) clatter up and down nearby Russian Hill every day.

Separate cables, whirring around giant wheels at a central power station (opposite), pull San Francisco's treasured cable cars along four routes, ranging in length from the 9,050-foot Powell Street line to 21,500 feet on California Street. The cables, made of steel wire wrapped around a natural-fiber core, must be replaced every 75 to 250 days. The cars, which travel at top speeds of 9.5 m.p.h., advance when their operators grab onto the moving cable with a grip that fits into a slot beneath the rails. The power station, at Washington and Mason streets, houses the city's free cable-car museum, where the story of the cars and the system's inventor, Andrew Smith Hallidie, is told. The most popular line with tourists ends at the foot of Hyde Street at a turnaround (above) reminiscent of those once functioning in railroad roundhouses.

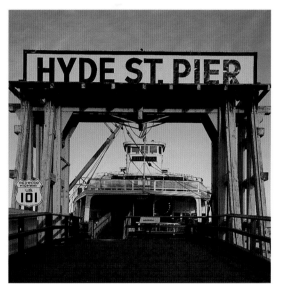

The Hercules *tugboat (left) and the old ferry boat* Eureka *at the Hyde Street Pier (above) are exhibits at the San Francisco Maritime National Historic Park near Fisherman's Wharf. The* Hercules *originally hauled lumber, then hay stacked more than twenty feet high on its decks, up and down the Pacific Coast before switching to heavy-duty tugboat chores on San Francisco Bay. Before bridges crossed the* Bay, the Eureka *was one of the ferries that connected U.S. 101— the "Redwood Highway"—between San Francisco and Sausalito. Built in 1890, it began service as the railroad ferry* Ukiah. *Uphill from the maritime museum is Ghirardelli Square (overleaf)— pronounced "GEAR-ar-delly— a shopping mecca in the 1900-vintage red-brick buildings of the old Ghirardelli chocolate factory.*

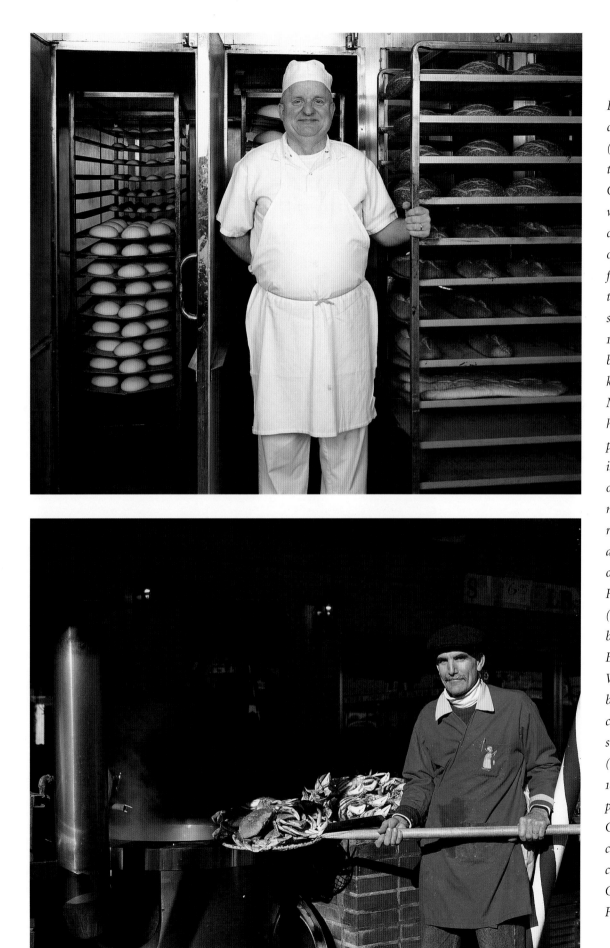

Locally owned chocolatier Confetti (opposite) is a key tenant at the Cannery, once the world's largest peach cannery and one of the nation's first factory buildings to be converted to a shopping center in the 1960s. Built in 1907 by a consortium later known as the Del Monte Company (see historic photograph on page 18), the Cannery is now home to one-of-a-kind shops—no chain operations—restaurants, galleries, and the Museum of the City of San Francisco. Willy Jaciw (top left) is the master baker at the Boudin Bakery's Fisherman's Wharf location. The bakery's specialty is classic San Francisco sourdough bread (see page 10 for an 1880s Boudin family portrait). Anthony Geraldi (bottom left) cracks and steams crabs at Fisherman's Grotto No. 9 at Fisherman's Wharf.

Dungeness crab—
served inside and
at a curbside steam
table—and cioppino,
a fish and shellfish
dish cooked with
tomatoes, wine, and
spices, are specialties
at Alioto's Restaurant
(above), a Fisherman's
Wharf institution run
by one of San Fran-
cisco's most prominent
families. Sea lions
mysteriously appeared
at Pier 39's west
marina (right) shortly
after the 1989 Loma
Prieta earthquake.

Each winter, as many
as six hundred vocifer-
ous adult males—
which can grow to 850
pounds—and adoles-
cent animals of both
sexes muscle for spots
on the floating docks.
Adult females stay
close to breeding
grounds as far away
as Baja California,
to which Pier 39's sea
lions migrate each
summer. Looking
north from the pier,
Alcatraz Island
(overleaf) is a short
ferry ride away.

Alcatraz. The word alone evokes stark images of desperate "cons" doing hard time in the bleak penitentiary in the middle of San Francisco Bay. From 1934 to 1963, Alcatraz Island was the home address to the "worst of the worst" federal prisoners, including Al Capone, George ("Machine Gun") Kelly, and Robert Stroud—the "Birdman of Alcatraz." Stroud actually never kept a canary on the island but earned his "Birdman" nickname previously at Leavenworth Penitentiary. In 1948, Frank Heaney (opposite), at age twenty-one, became the youngest man ever to serve on "The Rock." A born storyteller, Heaney—shown in the cellblock that the inmates wishfully called "Broadway"—later worked for the Blue & Gold ferry fleet, which carries more than a million visitors a year to the island. The burned-out warden's home (above) had earlier been an officers' club when Alcatraz was a military prison.

A "wave organ" (above) "plays" when one puts an ear to pipes embedded in stone and concrete at the point at the San Francisco Marina. An old lighthouse (right) stands on a spit of land nearby. Young Trevor Bulger, whose family was visiting from Vancouver, Washington, takes a turn inside a "listening vessel" (opposite) at the Exploratorium, a hands-on science museum housed in a pavilion of the Palace of Fine Arts. Looming overhead is a surviving angel from the 1915 Panama-Pacific Exposition for which the Palace of Fine Arts was constructed. The building's rotunda and peristyle were temporary lath, plaster, and chicken-wire affairs, designed by Bernard Maybeck. The palace gradually deteriorated and was replaced by a permanent concrete and steel landmark (overleaf) in the 1960s.

The Octagon House
(opposite) stands next
to a shady community
park in San Fran-
cisco's Cow Hollow
neighborhood—
named for the dairy
farms once located
there that supplied
most of the city's milk
and cheese. Now a
museum operated by
the National Society
of Colonial Dames,
it displays decorative
arts from the nation's
Colonial and Federal
periods. The house,
with its illuminated
cupola, was built
in 1861 by William
McElroy. It was one
of eight octagonal
homes built in town
at a time when it was
believed that eight-
sided houses provided
maximum light and
ventilation. Affluent
Pacific Heights boasts
grand homes such
as this mansion (top
left) with its mar-
velous topiary land-
scaping. Many homes
there and in Presidio
Heights feature lov-
ingly created Art Deco
details (lower left).

The Columbarium
(above) is a neo-
classical resting
place for cremated
remains built by the
Odd Fellows in 1865
in San Francisco's
Richmond District.
It was the center-
piece of a cemetery

whose plots were
moved to Daly City
after the 1906 earth-
quake to permit resi-
dential develop-
ment. The building
remained but was
abandoned from
1934 to 1979;
raccoons and birds

nested among the
urns. The Colum-
barium contains five
thousand niches—
many elegantly dec-
orated with stained-
glass windows and
treasured family
mementos and
houses the remains

of more than six
thousand people.
It was rehabilitated
when the Neptune
Society acquired the
facility. The Levan-
tine-style Temple
Emanu-El (oppo-
site), dedicated in
1926, features a

cloistered courtyard,
a bronze and enamel
ark fashioned like
an oversized jewel
box, great tapestries
and stained-glass
windows, and a 150-
foot-high dome that
can be seen across
much of the city.

The main campus of the University of San Francisco (above)— the city's oldest university—is located on a hill called "Lone Mountain" between Haight-Ashbury and Presidio Heights.

The Jesuit institution was founded in 1855, just six years after the great Gold Rush turned San Francisco from the sleepy Yerba Buena settlement into a boomtown that quickly became the

Queen City of the West. The 1914 Saint Ignatius Church serves the university and the surrounding community. In addition to its spectacular dome and campanile, it contains one of the city's most

beautiful sanctuaries (opposite). Its twin 210-foot towers are visible for miles, especially when they are lit at night. Because of its strong Asian, Hispanic, and even Russian influences, San Fran-

cisco boasts some of the nation's most diverse places of worship. Available are customized tours of Christian cathedrals, Jewish synagogues, and Chinatown temples.

One of San Francisco's distinctive houses of worship is the Roman Catholic Saint Mary's Cathedral (right) in the Western Addition. The 1971 building features four 190-foot hyperbolic paraboloids that form a Greek Cross above a gigantic sanctuary that seats twenty-five hundred people. The church replaced a previous Saint Mary's destroyed by fire. The one hundred-foot, five-tiered Peace Pagoda (opposite) was built in 1968 and announces the entrance to Japantown and the Japan Center, a large indoor mall. One of San Francisco's most familiar postcard views (overleaf)—capturing both nearby Victorian houses and the distant downtown skyline—is taken from Alamo Square at Fulton and Steiner streets. It lies in the heart of a historic district that contains many of the city's fourteen thousand "painted ladies" as the houses are affectionately called.

Ornamental pieces of many Queen Anne-style homes, including an 1890s house on Broderick Street (opposite), were ordered from catalogues. The Haas-Lilienthal House (left) in Pacific Heights is the only fully furnished San Francisco Victorian open to public tours. The Westerfield House (above) on Alamo Square was designed in 1889 by Henry Geilfuss in the "Stick" style made popular in Philadelphia. What appear to be visible support beams are purely decorative. More than fourteen thousand Victorian homes, of several styles, have been identified in San Francisco. Most are located west of Van Ness Avenue, where homes were dynamited to stop the spread of fires following the deadly 1906 earthquake.

It's been several
decades since cries
of "tune in, turn on,
drop out" echoed
throughout the
"summer of love" in
the hippie scene of San
Francisco's Haight-
Ashbury District. But

"flower power" is well
remembered in several
shops along Haight
Street. Positively
Haight Street (above)
is a colorful bead shop;
Wasteland (opposite)
sells vintage clothing
and eclectic party

supplies. "The Haight"
is still home to eccen-
tric coffee shops, cafés,
and "head shops"
selling marijuana
paraphernalia. And
young people with
multicolored coiffures
and ring-pierced

noses, lips, and
tongues still shuffle
along the street. It's
an almost nostalgic
scene that's not lost
on tour-bus operators
who drive visitors out
Haight Street regu-
larly. But the neigh-

borhood is carefully
watched by police and
has been largely
gentrified. Detached
"painted ladies" and
elegant row houses in
the Haight are now
among the city's most
desirable abodes.

The ornate Castro Theater (above)—built in 1923 as the flagship movie palace of the Nasser family chain—is a landmark in the Castro, the world's largest openly gay and lesbian neighborhood. Once a working-class Irish community, the Castro is famous for its impromptu celebrations, especially on Halloween. Its leaders wield considerable political clout at City Hall. A fixture is the Names Project storefront, where volunteers continue to sew sections of the giant quilt that memorializes AIDS victims. Refurbished F-line trolleys (right), obtained from Philadelphia and painted to salute seventeen cities where the streetcars once operated, run out of Market Street. Murals like Daniel Galvez's work (overleaf) above the House of Brakes—an appropriate setting in this city of steep hills—dot the Mission District south of Market Street.

The Franciscans'
Misíon San Francisco
de Asís, *today known
as Mission Dolores
(opposite), completed
in 1791, stands next
to the larger Mission
Dolores Basilica, built
in 1913. The oldest-
standing building
in San Francisco,
Mission Dolores was
once the northern ter-
minus of the Spanish
El Camino Real—
"royal way"—of
twenty-one missions
that stretched from
Southern California
in the eighteenth
century. Its adobe
walls and sequoia
beams withstood the
city's two significant
earthquakes well. In
back is a cemetery in
which five thousand
Native Americans—
whom Spanish mis-
sionaries subjugated
and attempted to
convert—are buried.
Down the street is
Dolores Park, marked
by a gateway bell
(left). With its play-
grounds, clubhouse,
and ample grounds
for strolling and
running dogs, it
is a centerpiece of
the city's Hispanic
community.*

The Conservatory of Flowers (above) is the oldest building in the city's luxuriant Golden Gate Park, which stretches from the Pacific Ocean to the middle of town. The city approached the great landscape architect Frederick Law Olmsted, designer of New York's Central Park and Boston's Public Gardens, to investigate the idea of this great urban park; he was skeptical that anything would grow atop the area's desolate sand dunes. W. H. Hall, a young San Franciscan, got the job done in the 1870s and the park became a city treasure. (For a historical view of the conservatory, see page 12.) James Lick's statue to Francis Scott Key (opposite) in the park's Botanical Gardens, completed in 1887, is inscribed with the words to "The Star-Spangled Banner." Golden Gate Park's favorite attraction is the Japanese Tea Garden (overleaf), built for the Midwinter Fair of 1894.

A Beach Chalet restaurant, through many incarnations, has stood at the west end of Golden Gate Park, welcoming visitors to the ocean-front. The original building was moved and later destroyed by arson. Its replacement, with the restaurant on the top floor and a public lounge and changing rooms below, opened in 1925. In the 1930s, French-born painter Lucien Labaudt was commissioned by the U.S. Works Progress Administration to complete fresco murals in the lounge area. One (opposite) depicts Fisherman's Wharf. Set high upon a sandy ridge, the new Golden Gate Park needed plenty of water to keep its fragile foliage green. First, wells were dug; then, around the turn of the twentieth century, two giant Dutch-style wind-mills were constructed and put in operation. Both survive, though neither functions, and only one (above) has giant vanes—by no means original.

The Cliff House (left), is the third in a series of gathering places overlooking Seal Rocks at Ocean Beach. The second, spanning the turn of the twentieth century, was a Victorian palace that attracted visitors in droves (see page 15 for a look at that colossus). The current Cliff House also offers food, libations, and an extensive gift shop. Downstairs is the Musée Méchanique, an enchanting collection of coin-operated mechanical marvels from old penny arcades. Included are player pianos, strength-testing machines, and animated characters like the fortune teller (above). All work. Admission is free, but the temptation to spend a few quarters playing the contraptions is irresistible.

This stone lion (above) and a companion are all that remain of Adolph Sutro's estate on Point Lobos above Ocean Beach. Engineer Sutro made a fortune financing a great Comstock Lode tunnel, and on his Cliff House and the "Sutro Baths" below his estate. An original cast of Auguste Rodin's The Thinker—and a magnificent pipe organ inside—welcome visitors to the California Palace of the Legion of Honor (right), a dramatic art museum whose collection spans four thousand years of ancient and European art. The building was given to San Francisco by Mr. and Mrs. Adolph Spreckels on Armistice Day, 1924, to honor Californians who died in World War I.

110

The onion-domed Holy Virgin Russian Orthodox Cathedral (opposite) is a reminder of the days when as many as ten thousand White Russians emigrated to San Francisco's Richmond District. They fled Russia after the Communist Revolution of 1917. The body of the parish's tireless founder, known as John the Barefoot, is displayed inside the cathedral. Earlier Russian seal and otter hunters based at Fort Ross farther north in California had sailed into San Francisco Bay but did not stay; Russian Hill, farther downtown, is said to have been named for two Russian seal hunters whose graves were discovered there. Residents of exclusive Seacliff (above), along the scenic El Camino del Mar, enjoy an exquisite view of the Golden Gate Bridge. And residents of Marin County, across the Bay, get a splendid view of the neighborhood's pastel-colored mansions.

Commissioned officers and their families, stationed at the Presidio U.S. Army base, lived in modest quarters on Officers' Row (left). Each little home had a privy, garden, and chicken coop. The homes were not electrified until 1912. The Presidio fortification dates to 1776, when a Spanish captain claimed the land for his country. Mexican troops took control but were ousted by Americans during the "Bear Flag Revolt" of 1846. Thereafter, the Presidio gained a reputation as the "country club" of military posts. On the grounds, about fifteen thousand American soldiers lie in the military cemetery, whose vistas are reminiscent of Arlington National Cemetery outside Washington. There's even a whimsical pet cemetery (above) nearby. Closed by Congress in 1994, the Presidio is now a sprawling National Park Service site.

Baker Beach (right), in the Presidio's southwest corner on the open ocean, is one of the city's most popular beaches and offers a fabulous view of the Golden Gate Bridge. Prudent visitors stay clear of the dangerous surf, though avid surf fishers stake out spots along it. Strollers often cannot resist climbing a rocky out-cropping—against which waves crash to add excitement to photographs—to get an even closer view of the bridge. Early-morning fog often envelopes the area, and the sun's dying rays accentuate the bridge's red-orange patina. In the warm-est months there is often another sight from these heights as well: nude sunbathers whose loitering is discouraged but not always curtailed. Overlooking the sand is a picnic area (above) shaded by Monterey pine and cypress trees.

Fort Point (opposite and above) hunkers beneath the southern anchorage of the Golden Gate Bridge, where an extra steel arch was added to protect the fort below. A fortification has guarded the Golden Gate since 1794, when the Spanish, using Native American labor, completed an adobe fort known as El Castillo de San Joaquin. *Mexico gained control after* its independence but abandoned El Castillo *in 1835. U.S. Army engineers placed a ten-gun battery on the bluff above in 1855 as Fort Point was being constructed from more* than eight million bricks and granite from California and China. The fort served as nerve center for construction of the Golden Gate Bridge (overleaf) between 1933 and 1937. Abandoned again, the fort was restored in the 1970s as a National Park Service site with extraordinary views of gun emplacements and the underbelly of the great bridge.

San Francisco is a distant vision (above) from Sausalito, the artsy Marin County community across the Golden Gate, where pelicans and seagulls gather on the rocks outside the Spinnaker Restaurant. Leisure is de rigueur at the artsy community's harbor (right), where yachts and houseboats dock. Like another fashionable Marin County community, Tiburon—once a railroad town to which whole trains were ferried from San Francisco—Sausalito was not always a trendy haven of boutiques, galleries, and coffee shops. A bootleggers' hideout during Prohibition, it was a grimy shipyard, full of roustabout bars, as recently as World War II. The work of more than one hundred artists is judged each September at the Sausalito Art Festival, where wines from Sonoma and Napa county vineyards are exhibited and sampled.

Stanford, near Palo Alto, is one of the region's outstanding universities. Its focal point is the 1903 Memorial Church (left), seen through the elaborate Main Gate. Blemished by both big Bay Area quakes, the chapel has been painstakingly reinforced and its decorative mosaics beautifully restored. Endowed by one of the area's "Big Four" railroad tycoons, Leland Stanford, the prestigious university suggests a sprawling mission complex. Named for conservationist John Muir, Marin County's Muir Woods (above)—home to spectacular old-growth coast redwoods—is now a national monument. One feature of a sweeping aerial view of the Golden Gate (overleaf) is Point Bonita, whose lighthouse is open weekends in season.

Index